GUINEA PIG MASTERY

Expert Care, Health, and Breeding Tips for Happy Pets

Berko Adofo

Table of Contents

INTRODUCTION

Guinea pigs, also known as cavies, are some of the most lovable and low-maintenance pets you can have. Their gentle nature, curious personalities, and adorable squeaks make them a joy to care for. Whether you're a first-time guinea pig owner or you're looking to deepen your knowledge of these delightful creatures, this guide will help you every step of the way.

Raising a guinea pig goes beyond just providing food and shelter—it's about creating a safe, enriching environment that supports their well-being. In this guide, you'll discover the essential aspects of guinea pig care, from understanding their nutritional needs to creating a comfortable habitat and even building a strong bond with your furry friend. Whether you're looking to ensure your guinea pig stays healthy, happy, and active or you're curious about their behavior and social needs, this book will serve as your ultimate resource for all things guinea pig. By the end, you'll have the knowledge and confidence to provide your guinea pig with the best care possible, ensuring they thrive in your home.

WELCOME TO THE GUINEA PIG WORLD

Welcome to the wonderful world of guinea pigs, where these tiny, furry companions bring endless joy, laughter, and affection into our lives. Guinea pigs are not just pets; they become part of the family, with their playful personalities and heartwarming antics. Whether you're thinking about adopting your first guinea pig or you're already a proud guinea pig owner, you're about to embark on an exciting journey of care, companionship, and discovery. In this guide, we'll take you through every aspect of guinea pig care, from setting up the perfect home to understanding their nutritional needs and health. Guinea pigs are gentle creatures with unique personalities, and with the right knowledge, you can create a safe, enriching environment where they'll thrive. So, let's dive in! Prepare to learn everything you need to know to ensure your guinea pig is happy, healthy, and well-cared for. From their diet and habitat to their quirky behaviors, we'll guide you through it all, helping you become the best guinea pig parent possible. Welcome to the world of guinea pigs, where love and joy await at every squeak and cuddle!

PURPOSE OF THIS GUIDE

The purpose of this guide is to provide you with a comprehensive resource for raising, feeding, and keeping your guinea pig healthy and happy. Whether you're a first-time pet owner or a seasoned guinea pig enthusiast, this guide is designed to equip you with the knowledge and confidence to care for these adorable and social animals.

Guinea pigs are sensitive creatures that require specific care to ensure they live long, healthy, and fulfilling lives. This guide aims to break down the essentials of guinea pig care in a way that's easy to understand, covering everything from proper housing and diet to grooming, handling, and recognizing signs of illness. By following the advice and tips in this guide, you'll learn how to create an environment that supports your guinea pig's physical and emotional well-being. We also aim to deepen your understanding of guinea pig behavior and social needs, ensuring that you can foster a strong, trusting bond with your pet. Ultimately, our goal is to help you become a responsible, loving guinea pig owner who can enjoy the unique joy these little animals bring into our lives.

WHO THIS BOOK IS FOR

This book is for anyone who is interested in raising and caring for guinea pigs, whether you're a first-time pet owner or someone looking to deepen your understanding of these charming creatures. If you're considering adopting a guinea pig or have recently welcomed one into your home, this guide will be your go-to resource for all things guinea pig care. It's also for those who want to provide the best environment for their pets, ensuring they live a long, healthy, and happy life. From novice owners seeking basic care instructions to experienced guinea pig enthusiasts wanting to enhance their knowledge, this book covers every aspect of guinea pig care—from feeding and housing to health and socialization. Additionally, this guide is for anyone interested in building a strong bond with their guinea pig, understanding their behaviors, and ensuring they feel safe and loved in your care. No matter your experience level, you'll find helpful advice, practical tips, and insights that will make you feel confident in your role as a guinea pig parent.

WHY GUINEA PIGS MAKE GREAT PETS

Guinea pigs are incredibly popular as pets, and for good reason. These small, gentle creatures have a host of qualities that make them great companions for people of all ages. Here are some reasons why guinea pigs make wonderful pets:

1. Gentle and Friendly: Guinea pigs are known for their calm and friendly nature. They are social animals that enjoy the company of humans and other guinea pigs. Unlike some pets, guinea pigs are less likely to bite or scratch, making them an ideal choice for families with children or first-time pet owners.

2. Low Maintenance: While guinea pigs do require care and attention, they are relatively easy to maintain compared to larger pets. Their simple dietary and habitat needs, along with their low grooming requirements, make them a manageable pet for busy individuals or families.

3. Interactive and Social: Guinea pigs are highly social animals that thrive on interaction and companionship. They love to communicate with their owners through sounds like squeaks and chirps, and they will often follow you around, excited to see you. Their playful behavior is sure to bring joy to your household.

4. Compact Size: Guinea pigs don't require a large living space, which makes them perfect for smaller homes or apartments. With the right cage setup and plenty of playtime outside their habitat, guinea pigs can happily live in even the smallest of spaces.

5. Non-Destructive: Guinea pigs are not destructive pets. They won't chew on furniture or dig up your yard, making them ideal for those looking for a pet that won't cause damage to their home.

6. Long Lifespan: Guinea pigs live for 5 to 7 years on average, which gives owners plenty of time to develop a close bond. This lifespan allows for a long-term relationship, making them a pet that grows with you and your family.

7. Entertaining: Guinea pigs are full of personality and will often entertain you with their curious behavior, adorable squeaks, and joyful leaps. Watching them interact with each other and explore their environment is both amusing and heartwarming.

8. Therapeutic Companionship: Their calming presence can have therapeutic benefits. Studies show that spending time with guinea pigs can help reduce stress, improve mood, and promote relaxation. Their soothing sounds and affectionate nature make them great companions for emotional well-being.

Overall, guinea pigs are affectionate, entertaining, and easy to care for, making them ideal pets for anyone looking for a low-maintenance but loving companion.

CHAPTER ONE

GETTING TO KNOW GUINEA PIGS

What Are Guinea Pigs?

Guinea pigs, also known as cavies, are small, herbivorous rodents that are native to the Andean region of South America. They are known for their docile, gentle nature and their love for companionship. Unlike pigs, guinea pigs are not actually pigs at all—they belong to the family Caviidae, which includes other species of rodents. They are social animals that thrive in groups, and in the wild, they live in herds for protection and companionship. Guinea pigs are easy to identify with their round bodies, short to long fur, and distinctively large, expressive eyes. These small creatures come in a variety of breeds and colors, with some having smooth coats and others sporting long, flowing fur. Despite their small size, they have big personalities, often expressing themselves through squeaks, purrs, and other vocalizations.

HISTORY AND ORIGINS OF GUINEA PIGS

Guinea pigs have a rich history that dates back thousands of years. They were first domesticated by the indigenous peoples of the Andes mountains in South America, where they have been kept as pets and livestock for food. The earliest evidence of guinea pigs being raised dates back over 3,000 years. In their natural habitat, guinea pigs were hunted for food and also served as ritualistic animals in various cultures. However, they were eventually domesticated due to their peaceful nature, ease of care, and their use in traditional medicine. By the 16th century, guinea pigs were introduced to Europe, likely through Spanish explorers, and became popular as pets in households across the continent.

Interestingly, guinea pigs are not found in the wild outside of South America. They are domesticated animals that rely on humans for food and shelter.

POPULARITY AND APPEAL AS PETS

Guinea pigs have gained immense popularity around the world as pets due to their friendly and gentle demeanor. Their small size, manageable care requirements, and social nature make them ideal companions for families, singles, and elderly individuals alike. They have become especially favored by those living in apartments or smaller spaces because they don't require large living areas. One of the primary appeals of guinea pigs as pets is their ability to form strong bonds with their owners. They enjoy interaction and can be trained to respond to their names or follow basic commands. Their vocalizations, such as purring and chirping, further enhance their charm and make them endearing to pet owners. Additionally, guinea pigs are known for their relatively low-maintenance needs. While they do require daily care, their simple diet of hay, fresh vegetables, and a clean living space makes them easier to care for than many other pets, such as dogs or cats.

COMMON MYTHS AND MISCONCEPTIONS

While guinea pigs are beloved by many, there are still some common myths and misconceptions surrounding them. Let's clear up a few of these:

1. Guinea Pigs are Pigs: Despite their name, guinea pigs are not pigs. They are rodents and have no relation to pigs. Their name comes from early European explorers who believed they came from Guinea (a region in Africa), and "pig" was used to describe their shape and squeaky sounds.

2. Guinea Pigs are Low Maintenance: While guinea pigs are easier to care for than some pets,

they still require daily attention. They need fresh hay, vegetables, a clean cage, and social interaction. They also need regular grooming, especially long-haired breeds.

3. Guinea Pigs Live Alone: Guinea pigs are very social creatures and thrive in groups. It's always best to adopt at least two guinea pigs so they can keep each other company and reduce loneliness. They can form deep bonds with each other and their human caregivers.

4. Guinea Pigs Can Live in a Small Cage: Guinea pigs need plenty of space to move around. A small, cramped cage can lead to stress and health issues. It's important to provide them with a spacious cage and ample playtime outside their habitat.

5. Guinea Pigs Don't Need Regular Vet Check-ups: Like any pet, guinea pigs require regular veterinary care. They are prone to certain health

issues, such as dental problems, respiratory infections, and gastrointestinal issues, and routine check-ups are essential for their well-being. By dispelling these myths and understanding the true nature of guinea pigs, you can provide them with the care and attention they truly deserve.

PREPARING FOR YOUR GUINEA PIG

Choosing the Right Guinea Pig for You

Before bringing a guinea pig into your home, it's important to understand the different breeds and personalities of these charming creatures. Guinea pigs come in various shapes, sizes, and coat types, which can influence how much care and grooming they require.

1. Consider Your Space: If you live in a smaller space, you might want to choose a breed that requires less grooming, such as the American or

Abyssinian guinea pig. These breeds have shorter fur compared to long-haired varieties like the Peruvian or Silkie, which require more frequent grooming.

2. Age of the Guinea Pig: While baby guinea pigs are adorable, they require a lot of care and attention to ensure they are properly socialized. Some new owners may prefer adopting an adult guinea pig, as they tend to be calmer and already accustomed to human interaction.

3. Single or Pair: Guinea pigs are highly social animals and thrive in the company of other guinea pigs. It is often best to adopt two guinea pigs at once so they can bond and keep each other company, reducing loneliness and stress. Make sure both guinea pigs are of the same sex unless you plan on breeding.

4. Rescue or Breeder: Consider adopting from a guinea pig rescue organization. There are many

guinea pigs in need of loving homes, and adopting from a rescue helps provide a second chance for these pets. If you choose to purchase from a breeder, ensure that they are responsible and prioritize the health and well-being of the animals.

SELECTING A HEALTHY GUINEA PIG

When selecting a guinea pig, it's important to make sure you're bringing home a healthy pet. Here are some tips to ensure the guinea pig you choose is in good condition:

1. Check for Clear Eyes: Healthy guinea pigs should have bright, clear eyes with no discharge or redness.

2. Look for Clean Fur: The coat should be shiny and clean, without any bald patches, parasites, or visible skin problems. Long-haired breeds should have well-groomed coats.

3. Observe Their Behavior: A healthy guinea pig will be alert, curious, and active. They should not appear lethargic or show signs of disinterest in their surroundings. Guinea pigs are social and will often approach you, especially if they are used to human contact.

4. Check for Signs of Illness: Look for symptoms like runny noses, coughing, wheezing, or diarrhea. These are signs that a guinea pig may be unwell and should be avoided until they receive proper care.

5. Body Condition: Gently handle the guinea pig to check for a healthy weight. A healthy guinea pig will have a firm, slightly rounded body, and you should not feel their bones jutting out.

UNDERSTANDING GUINEA PIG BEHAVIOR

Guinea pigs are very social and have their own unique ways of communicating with you and each other. Understanding their behavior will help you better care for them and strengthen your bond. Here are a few common guinea pig behaviors to look out for:

1. Squeaking and Chirping: Guinea pigs use a range of vocalizations to communicate. A loud, high-pitched squeak often signals excitement, such as when they are anticipating food or playtime. Chirping is a more unusual sound, often made by a guinea pig when they are in an unfamiliar or stressful situation.

2. Purring: A guinea pig's purr can mean several things. If your guinea pig is purring while you are petting them, it usually indicates contentment. However, if the purring is accompanied by other signs of discomfort, it may be a sign of pain or distress, so always pay attention to the context.

3. Popcorning: This is one of the cutest guinea pig behaviors. When they're feeling particularly

happy or excited, guinea pigs may jump in the air, often in a spontaneous "popcorn" motion. It's a sign that your guinea pig is full of energy and feeling safe and joyful.

4. Chasing and Nipping: Guinea pigs are territorial animals, and some may engage in chasing or nipping behavior, especially if they feel threatened or during the establishment of dominance in a group. Understanding guinea pig social dynamics can help prevent conflicts and create a peaceful environment.

5. Burying in Bedding: Guinea pigs love to burrow and hide in their bedding. This is a natural behavior that provides them with a sense of security. Ensure that they have enough bedding material to feel safe and comfortable.

PREPARING YOUR HOME FOR YOUR NEW PET

Setting up your home properly is crucial to ensuring your guinea pig's health and happiness. Before bringing your new pet home, make sure you have the right supplies and have created a comfortable environment for them to thrive in.

1. Choosing a Cage: Guinea pigs need a spacious cage to move around in. A minimum cage size of 7.5 square feet is recommended for two guinea pigs. The cage should have high sides to prevent bedding from being kicked out, and a solid floor is crucial for their safety (avoid wire-bottom cages, which can cause injury to their feet).

2. Bedding: Choose a safe bedding material like shredded paper or aspen shavings. Avoid cedar and pine bedding, as they can release harmful fumes. Your guinea pig will need soft, absorbent bedding to feel comfortable and stay clean.

3. Food and Water: Guinea pigs need constant access to fresh hay, vegetables, and clean water. Make sure to provide a water bottle or bowl that is easy for them to drink from, and replenish their food daily to keep them healthy.

4. Hideaways and Toys: Guinea pigs are curious creatures and need enrichment to stay active and mentally stimulated. Provide hideaways, tunnels, and chew toys to encourage exploration and satisfy their natural instincts.

5. Temperature and Lighting: Guinea pigs are sensitive to extreme temperatures. Aim to keep their environment at a comfortable temperature between 65-75°F (18-24°C). Keep their cage in a well-lit area, but avoid placing them in direct sunlight or in drafty areas. By taking the time to carefully prepare your home and understand your guinea pig's needs, you'll be setting up a positive and loving environment where your new pet can thrive. The more you know about guinea pigs and

their behavior, the easier it will be to ensure they live a happy, healthy life with you.

SETTING UP THE PERFECT GUINEA PIG HABITAT

Choosing the Right Cage

Choosing the right cage is one of the most important steps in setting up a safe and comfortable home for your guinea pig. The cage will be their primary living space, so it needs to be spacious, secure, and easy to clean. Here are some key factors to consider when selecting a cage:

1. Material: Guinea pig cages should have a solid floor and sturdy, chew-proof bars. Avoid cages with wire floors, as these can cause foot injuries and discomfort. Look for cages made from durable materials like plastic or metal that can withstand the guinea pig's chewing tendencies.

2. Type of Cage: There are two main types of guinea pig cages:

Pre-made cages: These cages come in various sizes and are easy to set up. They're convenient but may not always be large enough for two or more guinea pigs.

DIY Cages: Some guinea pig owners opt to build their own custom cage using materials like C&C grids (cubes and connectors) for more flexibility in size and layout. This option allows you to create a larger space and customize the habitat to suit your pet's needs.

3. Accessibility: Choose a cage with wide, easy-to-open doors to make it simple to access your guinea pig for cleaning, feeding, and petting. Large doors are also helpful when you need to move your guinea pig in and out of the cage.

CAGE SIZE AND LAYOUT

The size of the cage is crucial to your guinea pig's well-being. A small, cramped cage can lead to stress, boredom, and even health problems. Here's what you need to know about cage size and layout:

1. Recommended Cage Size: The minimum recommended cage size for a single guinea pig is 7.5 square feet (e.g., 30 inches by 36 inches), but the more space you can provide, the better. If you have two guinea pigs, aim for at least 10.5 square feet of space (e.g., 30 inches by 50 inches). The more room they have to move around, the healthier and happier they will be.

2. Multiple Levels: Guinea pigs enjoy exploring and need plenty of space to roam. If possible, choose a cage with multiple levels to increase the available floor space. You can also add ramps or

platforms to create more vertical space for them to explore.

3. Layout Tips: The layout of the cage should include designated areas for eating, sleeping, and playing. Place food and water bowls in a stable, easy-to-reach area. Ensure there's a separate space for their hideaway where they can retreat when feeling stressed or sleepy. You can also create areas for foraging and play with toys and tunnels.

4. Safety: Make sure the cage is secure, with bars that are spaced close enough together to prevent your guinea pig from squeezing through. The bars should also be chew-proof to prevent them from gnawing on the cage itself.

BEDDING AND SUBSTRATE OPTIONS

The bedding you choose plays a significant role in your guinea pig's comfort, health, and cleanliness.

Guinea pigs spend most of their time on the floor of their cages, so it's essential to use bedding that is safe, absorbent, and easy to clean. Here are some popular bedding options:

1. Shredded Paper Bedding: Shredded paper bedding is one of the safest and most absorbent options for guinea pigs. It is soft, comfortable, and helps control odors. Look for brands that are dust-free to prevent respiratory issues.

2. Aspen Shavings: Aspen is a safe alternative to cedar or pine bedding, which can release harmful fumes. Aspen shavings are absorbent and relatively inexpensive, making them a popular choice. Just be sure to choose unscented varieties, as strong scents can irritate your guinea pig's respiratory system.

3. Fleece Bedding: Fleece is a popular bedding option because it's washable and reusable, making it environmentally friendly. Fleece provides a soft

surface and can be paired with absorbent liners to keep the cage dry. However, it requires regular cleaning to avoid odor buildup.

4. Paper-based Bedding: Brands like Carefresh offer paper-based bedding that is highly absorbent and made from recycled materials. It's a great option for guinea pigs with sensitive respiratory systems and is gentle on their feet.

5. Avoid Cedar and Pine: These types of bedding release aromatic oils that can be harmful to guinea pigs, particularly to their respiratory health. Always avoid cedar and pine shavings when choosing bedding.

CREATING A SAFE AND STIMULATING ENVIRONMENT

Guinea pigs need more than just a place to sleep—they require a stimulating environment to keep them mentally and physically active. Here are some tips for creating a safe and enriching environment for your guinea pig:

1. Hideaways and Shelters: Guinea pigs are prey animals, so they need a safe place to hide when they feel scared or want to sleep. Provide small tunnels, cardboard boxes, or commercially available hideaways. You can also use soft fabric tents or wooden houses.

2. Exercise and Play Areas: Guinea pigs need space to run, explore, and exercise. Set up an exercise pen or use safe, guinea pig-friendly toys to encourage movement. You can use tunnels, balls, and chew toys to keep them entertained and active.

3. Chew Toys: Guinea pigs' teeth grow continuously, so providing chew toys is essential for their dental health. Look for chew sticks, wooden toys, or even cardboard to help keep their teeth trimmed and healthy. Avoid plastic chew

toys, as they can break into small pieces and cause choking hazards.

4. Foraging Opportunities: Guinea pigs are natural foragers, so providing opportunities for them to dig and search for food is important. You can hide small amounts of food in their bedding or scatter hay around the cage to encourage foraging behavior.

5. Interaction with Humans: Guinea pigs thrive on companionship, not only from other guinea pigs but from their human caregivers as well. Spend time with them daily, talking to them, petting them, or allowing them to sit on your lap. Guinea pigs love interaction, and the more time you spend with them, the more bonded they will become.

ESSENTIAL ACCESSORIES FOR GUINEA PIGS

In addition to a cage, bedding, and food, there are a few essential accessories that will help make your guinea pig's habitat more comfortable and functional:

1. Food and Water Bowls: Invest in sturdy, heavy food and water bowls that can't be easily tipped over. Stainless steel bowls are a great option because they are durable and easy to clean.

2. Litter Box: Guinea pigs often like to use one corner of their cage as a bathroom. You can add a small, low-sided litter box filled with safe bedding, such as paper pellets, to encourage them to keep their living area clean.

3. Water Bottle: A water bottle with a metal nozzle is a hygienic way to provide your guinea pig with fresh water. Make sure the bottle is positioned in

a way that your guinea pig can easily access it, but it doesn't spill or drip.

4. Nail Clippers: Guinea pigs' nails grow quickly, so regular nail trimming is essential to prevent overgrowth and injury. Invest in a pair of guinea pig-specific nail clippers or human nail clippers.

5. Playpen: If you want to give your guinea pig extra space outside of their cage, a playpen or exercise pen is a great way to provide more freedom for them to run around. Make sure the pen is escape-proof and set it up in a safe area of your home.

By providing a spacious, safe, and stimulating environment, you'll help your guinea pig live a long, happy, and healthy life. The effort you put into creating the perfect habitat will make a world of difference for your new furry friend.

CHAPTER TWO

GUINEA PIG NUTRITION AND FEEDING

What to Feed Your Guinea Pig

Feeding your guinea pig the right foods is essential for their health and well-being. Guinea pigs are herbivores and need a balanced diet that includes a variety of fresh vegetables, fruits, high-quality hay, and specially formulated pellets. Here's a breakdown of what should make up their diet:

1. Hay: Hay is the foundation of your guinea pig's diet. It provides the necessary fiber to keep their digestive system functioning properly and helps wear down their continuously growing teeth. The best type of hay to offer is timothy hay, but you can also give them other types like meadow hay or oat hay. Fresh hay should be available to your

guinea pig at all times. Aim for about 75% of their diet to consist of hay.

2. Pellets: Guinea pig pellets are specially formulated to provide essential nutrients and minerals. Choose high-quality pellets that are free from added sugars, artificial colors, or preservatives. Look for pellets that contain fortified vitamin C because guinea pigs cannot produce this vitamin on their own. Pellets should only make up about 10-15% of your guinea pig's diet.

3. Fresh Vegetables: Vegetables should make up about 20% of your guinea pig's diet. They love leafy greens such as romaine lettuce, cilantro, parsley, and dandelion greens. You can also offer vegetables like bell peppers, cucumbers, carrots, and zucchini. However, avoid iceberg lettuce, as it contains little nutritional value and may cause diarrhea.

4. Fresh Fruits: Fruits are a sweet treat for guinea pigs but should be given in moderation due to their high sugar content. Suitable fruits include apples, strawberries, kiwi, oranges, and blueberries. Be sure to remove any seeds or pits from fruits like apples, as they can be harmful to guinea pigs.

Fresh Vegetables, Fruits, and Hay

1. Vegetables: Guinea pigs love a wide variety of vegetables. The best options are high in fiber and low in calcium. Leafy greens are excellent choices, and you can rotate different types to keep their diet interesting. Bell peppers are especially beneficial, as they are high in vitamin C.

Leafy greens: Kale, Swiss chard, spinach (in moderation due to oxalates), and romaine lettuce are good choices.

Root vegetables: Carrots and beets are great, but should be given sparingly due to their sugar content.

Non-leafy vegetables: Peas, zucchini, and cucumber are also healthy choices.

2. Fruits: While fruits can be high in sugar, they provide important vitamins and antioxidants. Some of the best fruits for guinea pigs include apple slices (without seeds), blueberries, and strawberries. Always feed fruits in small portions to avoid digestive upset.

3. Hay: Hay is crucial for your guinea pig's digestive health and dental care. It should make up the bulk of their diet, with timothy hay being the most common and beneficial type. Always provide fresh, high-quality hay, as old or dusty hay can cause respiratory issues. Ensure your guinea pig always has access to unlimited hay throughout the day.

THE IMPORTANCE OF VITAMIN C

Vitamin C is essential for guinea pigs because, unlike humans, they cannot produce it on their own. Deficiency in vitamin C can lead to a condition called scurvy, which is characterized by symptoms like lethargy, swollen joints, and skin issues. To ensure your guinea pig gets enough vitamin C:

1. Fresh Vegetables: Offer plenty of vitamin C-rich vegetables, such as bell peppers, parsley, and kale. These can help supplement their vitamin C intake naturally.

2. Supplemental Vitamin C: You can also give guinea pig-specific vitamin C supplements in the form of tablets or drops, particularly if your pet is a picky eater. However, always consult with a vet before adding supplements to their diet.

3. Fortified Pellets: Choose guinea pig pellets that are fortified with vitamin C. This will ensure they are getting an additional source of this essential vitamin, but it shouldn't replace fresh foods like vegetables and fruits.

WATER AND FOOD BOWLS VS WATER BOTTLES

Proper hydration is crucial to your guinea pig's health. When it comes to providing water, there are two main options: water bowls and water bottles.

1. Water Bowls: Some guinea pigs prefer drinking from water bowls, as they are more natural and easier to access. A sturdy, heavy ceramic bowl will prevent spills and tipping. Make sure to clean the bowl daily to prevent bacteria buildup. If you use a water bowl, check it frequently to ensure it's always filled with fresh water.

2. Water Bottles: Water bottles with metal nozzles are a common choice because they prevent the water from spilling and keep the cage cleaner. However, some guinea pigs may not understand how to use them at first. Make sure the nozzle is clean and working properly to ensure your guinea pig is getting enough water. In either case, make sure fresh water is available to your guinea pig at all times. Guinea pigs can drink a significant amount of water each day, especially when consuming fresh vegetables, so it's important to monitor their hydration closely.

AVOIDING COMMON FEEDING MISTAKES

1. Overfeeding Sugary Foods: While guinea pigs enjoy fruits and some vegetables, they should only be given in moderation. Too many sugary treats can lead to obesity, dental problems, or digestive issues like diarrhea.

2. Feeding Too Much Fruit: Fruits are high in sugar, so it's essential to limit them. Offer small portions, no more than 1-2 tablespoons per day, and always remove any seeds or pits that could be dangerous.

3. Ignoring Fresh Hay: Never underestimate the importance of hay. A diet without enough hay can lead to severe digestive and dental problems. Always ensure there is plenty of hay available at all times.

4. Offering Unsafe Foods: Some foods can be toxic to guinea pigs. Avoid feeding them onions, garlic, potatoes, tomatoes (unripe or in excess), and chocolate. Always research a food before offering it to your guinea pig, as some seemingly harmless foods can be harmful.

5. Inconsistent Feeding Schedule: Guinea pigs thrive on consistency. Establish a regular feeding routine for fresh vegetables, hay, and pellets.

Feeding at the same times every day helps them feel secure and prevents overfeeding or underfeeding. By following these guidelines for guinea pig nutrition and feeding, you will help ensure that your furry friend remains healthy, happy, and well-nourished. Always monitor their diet and make adjustments as needed to suit their individual preferences and health needs.

GUINEA PIG HEALTH AND HYGIENE

Signs of a Healthy Guinea Pig

A healthy guinea pig is active, alert, and engaging with its environment. Here are some key indicators of a healthy guinea pig:

1. Clear Eyes and Ears: Healthy guinea pigs should have bright, clear eyes and clean ears. Any discharge or redness in the eyes or ears could be a sign of an infection or illness.

2. Normal Appetite: A guinea pig with a healthy appetite will regularly eat hay, vegetables, and pellets. A sudden decrease in food or water intake can be an indication of a health issue.

3. Active and Alert: Guinea pigs are naturally curious and social animals. A healthy guinea pig will move around its cage, explore, and interact with its environment. If your guinea pig is lethargic, it may be a sign of illness or stress.

4. Smooth, Shiny Coat: A healthy guinea pig's coat should be shiny, smooth, and free of bald patches. An unhealthy coat or excessive shedding could indicate skin problems or nutritional deficiencies.

5. Normal Breathing: Guinea pigs should breathe quietly and evenly. Labored or noisy breathing can be a sign of respiratory issues, which are common in guinea pigs.

6. Clean Bottom: A healthy guinea pig will have a clean bottom and be free of excessive wetness or

fecal buildup, which could signal digestive issues or diarrhea.

7. Social Behavior: Guinea pigs are social creatures. A healthy guinea pig enjoys interacting with you and its cage mates. Avoidance or aggressive behavior could be a sign of distress or illness.

COMMON GUINEA PIG HEALTH ISSUES

While guinea pigs are generally healthy animals, they can be prone to certain health conditions. Being aware of common health issues can help you catch them early and seek proper care.

1. Respiratory Infections: Guinea pigs are susceptible to respiratory issues, particularly if they are exposed to poor ventilation, dust, or drafty environments. Symptoms include sneezing, nasal discharge, wheezing, and difficulty breathing. If you notice any of these signs, consult

a vet immediately, as respiratory infections can be serious if left untreated.

2. Dental Problems: Guinea pigs' teeth grow continuously, so they need to chew on hay and other items to naturally wear them down. If they don't get enough fiber or the right kinds of foods, their teeth can become overgrown, leading to painful dental issues like malocclusion. Watch for signs of difficulty eating, drooling, or weight loss.

3. Diarrhea: Diarrhea can result from dietary changes, stress, or bacterial infections. If your guinea pig experiences diarrhea, ensure they are eating a balanced diet, and consider consulting a vet if it persists for more than 24 hours.

4. Urinary Issues: Guinea pigs may develop urinary tract infections or bladder stones. Symptoms include difficulty urinating, blood in urine, or frequent urination. If you notice any of

these signs, it's important to seek veterinary care promptly.

5. Skin Problems: Guinea pigs are prone to skin conditions like fungal infections, mites, or fungal ringworm. Look for excessive scratching, hair loss, or scabs. Regular grooming and maintaining a clean environment can help prevent many of these issues.

6. Bloating or Gas: Guinea pigs are also susceptible to digestive issues like bloating, which can be caused by poor diet, stress, or infections. This can be life-threatening if not treated quickly, so seek immediate veterinary attention if your guinea pig shows signs of abdominal discomfort, like a bloated stomach or reluctance to eat.

PREVENTATIVE CARE AND REGULAR VET CHECKUPS

Regular vet checkups are an essential part of maintaining your guinea pig's health. Here's what to keep in mind for preventative care:

1. Annual Checkups: It's important to take your guinea pig to the vet for a routine checkup at least once a year. Your vet will check for signs of illness, dental issues, skin problems, and overall health. They can also offer vaccination recommendations if necessary.

2. Dental Care: Since guinea pigs' teeth grow continuously, regular monitoring and checkups are crucial. If you notice your guinea pig having trouble eating or showing signs of dental discomfort, a vet may need to file or trim their teeth.

3. Parasite Prevention: Guinea pigs can contract external parasites, like fleas, mites, or lice.

Regularly check your guinea pig for any signs of parasites, especially if they are scratching or losing fur. Your vet can recommend appropriate treatments or preventative measures.

4. Vaccinations: Although guinea pigs don't require regular vaccinations like some other pets, there are certain vaccines that may be recommended by your vet, depending on your geographic location and lifestyle.

5. Weight Management: Obesity is a common issue in guinea pigs, particularly those that are overfed or not provided with enough space to exercise. Monitor your guinea pig's weight and adjust their diet and exercise routine as needed.

GROOMING BRUSHING, BATHING, AND NAIL TRIMMING

Proper grooming is essential for keeping your guinea pig comfortable, clean, and healthy. Here are some basic grooming tasks to keep in mind:

1. Brushing: Regular brushing helps keep your guinea pig's coat healthy and free of tangles. Short-haired guinea pigs need less frequent brushing (once a week), while long-haired guinea pigs require more regular grooming to prevent mats and tangles. Be gentle, and use a soft brush specifically designed for small animals.

2. Bathing: Guinea pigs don't require regular baths, as they are naturally clean animals. Over-bathing can strip their skin of essential oils and cause dryness. Only bathe your guinea pig if necessary, such as when they get very dirty or develop skin issues. Use a gentle, guinea pig-safe

shampoo and ensure their coat is thoroughly dried afterward.

3. Nail Trimming: Regular nail trimming is essential to prevent overgrowth, which can cause pain or difficulty walking. Use specialized guinea pig nail clippers and trim a small amount off each nail every 3-4 weeks. Be careful not to cut too close to the quick, which can cause bleeding. If you're unsure, ask a vet or groomer to show you the proper technique.

DEALING WITH SHEDDING AND COAT CARE

Guinea pigs naturally shed their fur throughout the year, especially during seasonal changes. Here's how to manage shedding and keep their coat in top condition:

1. Regular Brushing: Regular brushing helps reduce shedding and prevents hairballs from forming. It's also a great bonding activity with

your guinea pig. Long-haired guinea pigs require more frequent grooming to maintain their coat and prevent tangles.

2. Healthy Diet: A balanced diet rich in fiber, vitamins, and minerals is essential for a shiny, healthy coat. Make sure your guinea pig is getting plenty of fresh hay, vegetables, and vitamin C to keep their fur looking its best.

3. Environmental Factors: Dry or overly hot environments can cause excessive shedding. Make sure your guinea pig's habitat is in a comfortable, temperature-controlled area with adequate humidity levels.

By maintaining proper health, hygiene, and grooming routines, you can help your guinea pig live a long, happy, and comfortable life. Regular attention to their physical needs, along with a healthy diet and environment, ensures that your guinea pig remains content and thriving.

CHAPTER THREE

HANDLING AND SOCIALIZING YOUR GUINEA PIG

How to Handle Your Guinea Pig Safely

Guinea pigs are gentle animals, but they can be skittish, especially if they are not accustomed to handling. It's important to approach them with care and patience. Here's how to handle your guinea pig safely:

1. Approach Slowly and Calmly: Guinea pigs can easily startle, so always approach them slowly and calmly. Speak softly to let them know you're there, and avoid sudden movements that might scare them.

2. Support Their Body: When picking up your guinea pig, always support its body. Place one hand under their chest and the other under their hindquarters to ensure they feel secure. Never

pick them up by the scruff or by their limbs, as this can cause injury.

3. Lift Them Gently: Once you have your guinea pig supported, gently lift them straight up, keeping their body close to yours. Hold them snugly, but not too tightly, so they feel safe and comfortable. Guinea pigs are prey animals, so they might feel insecure when elevated too high off the ground.

4. Hold Them Close: Guinea pigs are more likely to feel secure when held close to your body. Sit down in a quiet space, such as on a couch or floor, and hold your guinea pig gently against your chest. This way, they feel safe and are less likely to squirm or try to escape.

5. Never Drop Them: Guinea pigs can easily get injured if they fall, so never allow them to jump or escape from your hands. Always make sure they are supported while being handled.

6. Allow Them to Climb and Explore: Once your guinea pig is comfortable with handling, let them explore your hands or lap. This helps them get used to your touch and builds trust between you and your pet.

UNDERSTANDING GUINEA PIG BODY LANGUAGE

Guinea pigs communicate through their body language and vocalizations. Understanding these cues is essential for interpreting their emotions and needs. Here are some key body language signals to look for:

1. Relaxed Body: A calm and relaxed guinea pig will have a soft, relaxed posture. Their body will be flat, and their head will be in a neutral position. Their eyes will be wide open but not staring, and they may engage in calm activities such as chewing or exploring.

2. Ears Upright: When a guinea pig's ears are upright and facing forward, it generally indicates alertness or curiosity. They may be focusing on something in their environment.

3. Barking or Whining: Guinea pigs may make a "barking" sound or high-pitched squeaks when they are excited or startled. A whine, on the other hand, may indicate distress or discomfort. Always pay attention to the context in which these sounds occur.

4. Purring or Chutting: Guinea pigs often make a purring or chutting noise when they are content and comfortable. A soft purring sound indicates relaxation, whereas a louder, chattering sound can indicate happiness or excitement.

5. Teeth Chattering: When guinea pigs chomp their teeth or make a chattering sound, it can be a sign of agitation, discomfort, or a warning. It's their way of signaling that they are feeling

threatened or upset. Give them space and avoid handling them if you notice this behavior.

6. Hunched Body and Hiding: A guinea pig that is hunched over or hiding in a corner may be feeling anxious or unwell. This behavior can indicate stress or illness, so it's essential to monitor them closely for any signs of health issues.

7. Popcorning: Popcorning is a happy behavior that involves sudden, playful jumps or bounces. It's common in young guinea pigs or those that are very content. This is a fun way for your guinea pig to express excitement and joy.

BONDING WITH YOUR GUINEA PIG

Building a strong bond with your guinea pig takes time and patience, but it's an essential part of having a positive relationship with your pet. Here are some tips to help you bond:

1. Consistency: Guinea pigs thrive on routine. Spend time with them at the same time each day to establish a sense of security and predictability. The more consistent you are, the more your guinea pig will learn to trust you.

2. Gentle Touch: Approach your guinea pig gently and always handle them in a calm manner. Use soft, slow movements to avoid startling them. Consistent, gentle interactions will help your guinea pig feel safe in your presence.

3. Speak Softly: Guinea pigs are sensitive to noise. Speak softly to them during interactions. This helps create a calm atmosphere and allows your guinea pig to feel more at ease.

4. Let Them Explore: Allow your guinea pig to explore their environment on their own terms. This gives them the space they need to feel in control of their surroundings. You can also use

this time to interact with them by offering treats or engaging in gentle play.

5. Treats and Rewards: Offering healthy treats like fresh vegetables or small pieces of fruit can help you bond with your guinea pig. Just make sure to offer treats in moderation to maintain a balanced diet.

6. Trust Takes Time: It may take some time for your guinea pig to trust you fully. Allow them to come to you at their own pace, and don't force interactions. Building trust is a gradual process, but the results are worth the wait.

SOCIALIZATION WITH OTHER GUINEA PIGS

Guinea pigs are social animals, and they thrive in the company of other guinea pigs. However, not all guinea pigs will get along immediately. Here's how to encourage positive socialization:

1. Same-Sex Pairing: To avoid breeding, it's best to keep guinea pigs of the same sex together. Make sure both guinea pigs are of similar size and temperament for the best chances of a successful bond.

2. Young Guinea Pigs: Younger guinea pigs tend to be more adaptable to new friends. Pairing a baby guinea pig with an older one can help ease the transition, though supervision is still necessary.

3. Separate Spaces: When introducing guinea pigs, it's a good idea to keep them in separate cages at first. This allows them to get used to each other's scent and presence without the risk of immediate conflict.

4. Supervised Introductions: When you are ready for the guinea pigs to meet face-to-face, do so in a neutral space, such as a clean play area. Make sure the introduction is calm and supervised, and

keep an eye out for any signs of aggression, such as biting or chasing.

5. Signs of Compatibility: Guinea pigs that are compatible with each other will often groom one another, share food, and snuggle together. If there is consistent fighting or aggression, it may be necessary to separate them and consult with a vet or guinea pig expert for advice.

INTRODUCING NEW GUINEA PIGS TO EACH OTHER

Introducing new guinea pigs to your existing pets can be a delicate process, but it's important to do so carefully to avoid stress and conflict. Here's how to introduce them successfully:

1. Neutral Territory: When introducing a new guinea pig, choose a neutral area, free of any established territory. This helps to avoid territorial disputes, as guinea pigs are often protective of their own space.

2. Slow and Gradual: Let the guinea pigs interact gradually. Keep their cages close to each other at first so they can get used to one another's presence. Gradually increase the time they spend together under supervision.

3. Observe Their Behavior: Pay attention to how the guinea pigs react to each other. If there is any excessive fighting or chasing, separate them and try again later. It's important to give them time to adjust to each other's presence.

4. Ensure Plenty of Space: Make sure there is enough space for each guinea pig in the cage to avoid territorial disputes. They should each have access to food, water, and comfortable resting spots. By handling your guinea pig safely, understanding their body language, and encouraging positive socialization, you can build a strong bond with your pet and create a peaceful and enriching environment for both you and your guinea pig.

GUINEA PIG PLAY AND ENRICHMENT

The Importance of Mental Stimulation

Guinea pigs are intelligent, social animals that thrive on mental stimulation. Without sufficient enrichment, they can become bored, stressed, or even depressed. Just like physical exercise, mental activity is essential to a guinea pig's overall well-being. Here's why providing mental stimulation is so important:

1. Prevents Boredom: Guinea pigs that are not mentally stimulated can quickly become bored, leading to behavioral issues such as excessive chewing on cage bars or even self-harming behaviors like over-grooming.

2. Encourages Natural Behaviors: Providing enrichment encourages your guinea pig to engage in natural behaviors, such as foraging, exploring,

and problem-solving. This helps them feel more content and fulfilled.

3. Boosts Emotional Health: Mental stimulation plays a significant role in keeping your guinea pig happy. When they are mentally engaged, they are less likely to show signs of stress or anxiety, helping to maintain a positive emotional state.

4. Promotes Physical Activity: Mental stimulation often leads to physical activity. When guinea pigs are busy exploring or interacting with toys, they are more likely to move around, improving their physical health and fitness.

SAFE TOYS AND ACTIVITIES FOR GUINEA PIGS

Guinea pigs love to explore and play, but it's important to ensure that the toys and activities you provide are safe and suitable for them. Here are some ideas for safe and engaging toys and activities for your guinea pig:

1. Chew Toys: Guinea pigs need to chew to keep their teeth healthy, so providing chew toys is essential. Look for safe options made from natural wood, such as applewood or willow branches. Avoid toys with toxic paints or chemicals.

2. Foraging Toys: Guinea pigs enjoy foraging, so toys that allow them to search for food are great for mental stimulation. You can use puzzle feeders or hide small amounts of their favorite treats in hay or paper bags to encourage them to explore and find their food.

3. Cardboard Tubes and Boxes: Guinea pigs love to hide and explore in cardboard tubes or boxes. These inexpensive toys mimic the burrowing behavior that guinea pigs naturally enjoy. Just be sure the cardboard is non-toxic and free from harmful chemicals.

4. Balls and Rattles: Some guinea pigs enjoy rolling balls or rattles around their play area.

Choose soft plastic or rubber balls that are not too small, as guinea pigs may try to eat small pieces, which could pose a choking hazard.

5. Climbing Structures: Guinea pigs enjoy climbing and exploring, so providing a safe, low climbing structure can encourage physical activity. Use sturdy materials, and ensure that there are no sharp edges or small parts that could cause injury.

6. Soft Fabric Tunnels: Guinea pigs love to run through tunnels. Soft fabric tunnels provide a cozy space for your guinea pig to explore, hide, and rest. They also enjoy running through them during playtime. Ensure the fabric is durable and machine washable.

7. Wooden Blocks or Chewable Sticks: Wooden blocks, sticks, or untreated wicker balls are great for your guinea pig to chew on, helping to wear down their teeth while keeping them entertained.

8. Hanging Veggie Treats: Hanging fresh veggies, like leafy greens or carrot tops, from the side of their cage is a fun and interactive way to encourage foraging. It also helps keep your guinea pig physically active while providing a healthy snack.

CREATING A GUINEA PIG PLAY AREA

Creating a designated play area for your guinea pig can enhance their quality of life and give them the freedom to explore and interact with various toys and accessories. Here's how to set up the perfect guinea pig play zone:

1. Choose a Safe Space: The play area should be in a safe, enclosed space where your guinea pig cannot escape or get into danger. A playpen or a gated area within your home can provide a secure environment. If you have other pets, make sure to supervise playtime to prevent accidents.

2. Ensure Non-Slip Flooring: The surface of the play area should be non-slip to prevent your guinea pig from slipping and hurting themselves. Avoid tile or hardwood floors, which can be too slippery. Instead, opt for soft, safe materials such as towels, fleece, or guinea pig-friendly mats.

3. Provide Hiding Spots: Guinea pigs need a sense of security when they play. Incorporate small hideaways, such as cardboard boxes or tunnels, where your guinea pig can retreat if they feel overwhelmed or need to rest.

4. Add Obstacles and Tunnels: Create an engaging environment with obstacles for your guinea pig to explore. Low ramps, tunnels, or soft climbing structures are great ways to encourage movement and exploration.

5. Provide Fresh Hay: Make sure your guinea pig has access to fresh hay during playtime. Not only

will it encourage foraging, but it also serves as an important part of their diet.

6. Keep Play Sessions Short and Sweet: While guinea pigs enjoy playtime, it's important not to overwhelm them. Short sessions of 15-30 minutes of play, a few times a day, can be sufficient to keep them happy and active without tiring them out.

HOW TO KEEP YOUR GUINEA PIG ACTIVE AND ENGAGED

To keep your guinea pig engaged and physically active, it's important to vary their activities and routines. Here are some tips for maintaining their mental and physical well-being:

1. Interactive Play: Spend time interacting with your guinea pig daily. You can hand-feed them vegetables, encourage them to explore new toys, or engage in gentle play. Interaction builds your bond and provides valuable mental stimulation.

2. Rotate Toys: Guinea pigs, like most animals, can get bored if they have access to the same toys all the time. Rotate their toys every few days to keep things fresh and exciting. This helps maintain their interest and encourages more exploration.

3. Foraging Time: Hide treats or fresh veggies in their cage or play area to simulate a natural foraging experience. Use hay, paper bags, or small plastic containers to make it more interesting and to encourage them to move around.

4. Exercise and Exploration: Allow your guinea pig to explore different parts of your home (in a safe and supervised manner) or let them roam in a playpen. This gives them the chance to explore new environments and engage in natural behaviors like burrowing, climbing, or running.

5. Vary Their Environment: Change the layout of their cage or play area from time to time. This

keeps them mentally engaged and helps avoid monotony. Guinea pigs enjoy discovering new things, so rearranging their space can provide hours of entertainment.

6. Companionship: Guinea pigs are social animals that benefit from the company of other guinea pigs. If possible, consider adopting a second guinea pig to provide companionship. Social play and interaction are excellent ways to keep your guinea pig active, engaged, and happy. By incorporating a variety of toys, activities, and interactive play, you can ensure your guinea pig remains mentally and physically stimulated. A well-enriched guinea pig will be healthier, happier, and more relaxed in their environment.

CHAPTER FOUR

GUINEA PIG BREEDING AND REPRODUCTION

Understanding Guinea Pig Reproduction

Guinea pig reproduction is a fascinating process, but it requires careful planning and knowledge to ensure the health and well-being of both the parents and the pups. Understanding the basic principles of guinea pig reproduction is crucial for anyone considering breeding these adorable creatures.

1. Sexual Maturity: Guinea pigs reach sexual maturity at different ages depending on their sex. Female guinea pigs (sows) can become sexually mature as early as 4 weeks old, but it is recommended to wait until they are at least 4-6 months old before breeding to ensure they are physically mature. Male guinea pigs (boars) can

become sexually mature at around 3-4 months old.

2. Reproductive Cycle: Female guinea pigs do not have a regular estrous cycle like many other animals. Instead, they come into heat (estrus) every 15-17 days, but they are only receptive to mating for about 6-12 hours during this period. Signs of estrus include restlessness, increased vocalizations, and a more noticeable arch in their back when touched.

3. Mating Behavior: When a female guinea pig is in heat, she may exhibit mating behaviors such as chirping, mounting, or displaying a "popcorning" dance. Male guinea pigs are generally more vocal and active during this time, often making a series of purring or wheeking sounds to attract a mate.

4. Pregnancy: Once mating has occurred, the female guinea pig may become pregnant. The gestation period for guinea pigs is around 59-72

days, one of the longest in rodents. It's important to know that guinea pigs can get pregnant again immediately after giving birth, so care must be taken to prevent unplanned litters.

PREPARING FOR BREEDING

Before breeding guinea pigs, thorough preparation is essential to ensure the health and safety of the animals involved.

1. Health Checks: Both the male and female guinea pigs should undergo thorough health checks by a veterinarian before being bred. This includes checking for any signs of illness or genetic conditions that could affect the pregnancy or the health of the pups.

2. Choosing the Right Pair: When selecting guinea pigs for breeding, it's important to consider their temperament, size, and genetic health. Ideally, choose guinea pigs from a similar age range and size to ensure compatibility. Avoid breeding

guinea pigs with a history of genetic disorders or known health issues.

3. Breeding Environment: Set up a clean, quiet, and stress-free environment for the breeding pair. The female guinea pig should be housed in a spacious cage with access to plenty of food, water, and bedding. Avoid introducing any other animals into the space to reduce stress during the breeding process.

4. Breeding Schedule: Guinea pigs can breed year-round, but it is essential to ensure that both animals are ready for the process. Never breed animals that are too young or too old. Females over 6 months and under 2 years old are considered the ideal age for pregnancy.

MATING, PREGNANCY, AND BIRTH

Once the breeding pair is ready, understanding the mating, pregnancy, and birthing process is crucial.

1. Mating Process: When the female is in heat and ready to mate, the male will court her. If they successfully mate, the female may show signs of pregnancy within a week, such as weight gain, increased appetite, or a change in behavior. Mating may take place over several attempts.

2. Signs of Pregnancy: Pregnancy in guinea pigs can be detected after about 2-3 weeks. During this time, the sow will gradually gain weight, and you may notice changes in her body, including a swelling abdomen. You can also feel the pups moving around in her belly after 4-5 weeks of gestation. Pregnant guinea pigs may become more passive and seek additional food or rest.

3. Caring for a Pregnant Guinea Pig: It's important to provide the pregnant sow with a balanced diet that includes plenty of hay, fresh vegetables, and vitamin C. Make sure she has a quiet and stress-free environment where she can relax and prepare for the birth. Regular health check-ups with the vet are advisable to monitor the pregnancy's progress.

4. Giving Birth (Kindling): Guinea pigs typically give birth to 1-6 pups, with the average litter being 2-4. The birth process is generally quick and straightforward, although complications can sometimes occur. Most guinea pigs give birth without assistance, but it's essential to have a veterinarian available in case of any complications.

Pre-Birth Behavior: As the birth approaches, the female may become restless and may start to build a nest. She will likely move around the cage and show signs of nesting behavior.

The Birth Process: The birth itself is usually quick, with each pup being born in a sac. The mother will instinctively clean and care for each pup right after birth. If the mother shows signs of distress or if any pups are born without being cleaned, you should contact a veterinarian immediately.

5. Post-Birth Care: After giving birth, the mother will typically rest, and the pups will begin to nurse from her. It's crucial to monitor the mother's health and provide her with extra food, water, and comfort. If there are any signs of complications such as bleeding or excessive lethargy, consult a veterinarian immediately.

RAISING HEALTHY GUINEA PIG BABIES (PUPS)

Caring for guinea pig pups requires special attention to ensure they grow up healthy and strong.

1. The First Few Days: Guinea pig pups are born fully furred, with their eyes open and teeth developed. They are able to eat solid food immediately and will nurse from their mother for the first few weeks of life. During the first few days, monitor the pups to ensure they are nursing and gaining weight.

2. Weaning: Guinea pig pups are typically weaned at 3-4 weeks of age. However, they can continue to nurse until 6 weeks if desired. Once weaning begins, it's important to provide the pups with a nutritious diet of hay, fresh vegetables, and specially formulated guinea pig pellets. Make sure to offer plenty of water and supervise the transition to solid foods.

3. Socialization: Guinea pig pups should be handled gently from a young age to ensure they become well-socialized. Interacting with them daily will help them become accustomed to

humans and other guinea pigs, reducing fear and stress later in life.

4. Health Checks: Regular health check-ups are important to monitor the development of the pups. Watch for signs of malnutrition, dehydration, or illness. Guinea pig pups should grow steadily, and if there are any concerns about their health, consult a veterinarian immediately.

ETHICAL CONSIDERATIONS IN GUINEA PIG BREEDING

Breeding guinea pigs should not be undertaken lightly, as it comes with serious ethical responsibilities.

1. Overpopulation Concerns: Guinea pigs are highly reproductive animals, and breeding should be done with the goal of improving the breed, not contributing to overpopulation. Consider adopting guinea pigs from shelters or rescues

instead of breeding, as many guinea pigs in shelters are in need of homes.

2. Genetic Health: Ethical breeders ensure that both the male and female guinea pigs are healthy and free from genetic disorders. Breeding should not be done to create animals with known health issues or defects, as this can lead to unnecessary suffering.

3. The Welfare of the Animals: Always prioritize the welfare of the guinea pigs involved in the breeding process. Make sure that the mother has adequate space, a balanced diet, and proper veterinary care throughout her pregnancy. Be prepared to provide ongoing support for the pups once they are born.

4. Considerations for New Owners: When breeding guinea pigs, it's important to ensure that the pups will be placed in responsible homes. Educate potential owners about the care needs of

guinea pigs and provide them with the resources they need to properly care for their new pets. Breeding guinea pigs can be a rewarding experience if done responsibly. However, it requires a deep understanding of their reproductive process, ethical considerations, and the time and resources needed to care for both the parents and the pups. By approaching guinea pig breeding with care, compassion, and education, you can contribute positively to the health and happiness of these wonderful animals.

TROUBLESHOOTING AND COMMON ISSUES

Dealing with Stress and Anxiety in Guinea Pigs

Guinea pigs are naturally gentle and social animals, but they can experience stress and anxiety, which can lead to health problems if not addressed. Understanding the signs of stress and taking action to mitigate it is crucial for your guinea pig's well-being.

1. Signs of Stress and Anxiety: Guinea pigs may show several signs of stress, such as excessive vocalization (whining, chattering), hiding, loss of appetite, trembling, or changes in behavior. If your guinea pig seems more withdrawn, is overeating, or is excessively scratching, it might be an indication that they are feeling anxious or stressed.

2. Common Causes of Stress: Several factors can contribute to stress in guinea pigs, including:

Environmental changes: Moving to a new home or cage, loud noises, or the introduction of new animals can unsettle guinea pigs.

Lack of socialization: Guinea pigs are social creatures and can become stressed if left alone for too long or if they are isolated from other guinea pigs.

Poor cage conditions: Overcrowding, lack of enrichment, dirty bedding, or inadequate hiding places can lead to anxiety.

Health issues: Physical discomfort or illness can contribute to a guinea pig's stress levels.

3. Reducing Stress:

Create a safe environment: Provide a quiet, comfortable space with plenty of hiding spots and a clean cage.

Regular handling and interaction: Regular, gentle handling can help your guinea pig feel more secure and bonded with you.

Social companionship: If possible, consider adopting another guinea pig for companionship, as they are herd animals and thrive in the company of other guinea pigs.

Consistent routine: Guinea pigs thrive on routine. Ensure they are fed, cleaned, and handled at the same time each day to provide predictability and security.

HANDLING AGGRESSION AND FEARFUL BEHAVIOR

While guinea pigs are typically friendly and peaceful, some may display signs of aggression or fearful behavior, especially when they are frightened or feel threatened.

1. Signs of Aggression: Aggressive guinea pigs may display behaviors such as:

Chasing or biting: This can happen during disputes with other guinea pigs or if they feel cornered or threatened.

Chattering teeth or lunging: A sign of aggression or defense, often seen when a guinea pig feels threatened or is trying to establish dominance.

Cage guarding: Some guinea pigs can be territorial and may become aggressive if they feel their space is being invaded.

2. Fearful Behavior: Guinea pigs may become fearful if they are subjected to loud noises, sudden movements, or rough handling. They may freeze, attempt to run, or try to hide in response to fear.

3. Addressing Aggression and Fear:

Gentle handling: Always approach your guinea pig calmly and avoid sudden movements or loud noises that could scare them.

Provide safe spaces: Ensure your guinea pig has hiding places where they can retreat to feel safe.

Proper socialization: Gradually introducing guinea pigs to new environments, people, or other guinea pigs can help reduce fear and aggression over time.

Understanding body language: Pay close attention to your guinea pig's body language. If they are chattering their teeth, hissing, or puffing up, it may indicate they are uncomfortable, and you should give them space.

COMMON HEALTH PROBLEMS AND TREATMENTS

Guinea pigs are generally healthy creatures, but like any pet, they can experience health issues. Being aware of the common health problems they face and knowing how to treat them is important for any guinea pig owner.

1. Respiratory Infections: Guinea pigs are susceptible to respiratory infections, which can result in symptoms like wheezing, nasal discharge, or labored breathing. These infections can be caused by environmental stress, poor hygiene, or a sudden change in temperature.

Treatment: Take your guinea pig to the vet for antibiotics and proper care. Ensure the living environment is clean, dry, and free of drafts.

2. Dental Problems: Guinea pigs have continuously growing teeth, and if they don't have enough fiber in their diet to wear them down, it can lead to dental problems such as overgrown teeth.

Symptoms: Difficulty eating, drooling, or noticeable teeth problems.

Treatment: Provide plenty of hay to encourage chewing. If teeth problems persist, a veterinarian may need to trim the teeth.

3. Gastrointestinal Issues: Guinea pigs can suffer from digestive problems, including bloating, diarrhea, or constipation, which can be caused by diet changes, stress, or infection.

Treatment: If symptoms persist for more than a day or two, consult a vet. Ensure your guinea pig is eating enough hay, fresh veggies, and drinking plenty of water.

4. Urinary Tract Infections (UTI): UTIs are common in female guinea pigs and can cause discomfort, frequent urination, or blood in the urine.

Treatment: A vet will prescribe antibiotics to treat UTIs. Keeping your guinea pig's cage clean and ensuring they drink enough water can help prevent infections.

COPING WITH ILLNESS AND INJURIES

If your guinea pig falls ill or sustains an injury, it's essential to act quickly and seek veterinary care. Guinea pigs are prey animals and tend to hide symptoms of illness, so it's important to monitor them closely.

1. Recognizing Signs of Illness: Some common signs that your guinea pig may be sick include:

Loss of appetite or weight loss

Change in behavior (becoming more lethargic or withdrawn)

Discharge from eyes or nose

Difficulty breathing or wheezing

Diarrhea or constipation

Changes in urine (color or frequency)

2. Treating Illness: Always seek veterinary attention if your guinea pig shows signs of illness. Do not attempt to treat them on your own unless advised by a professional. Ensure they have access to fresh water, a clean cage, and proper food while recovering.

3. Injuries: Guinea pigs can suffer from cuts, scrapes, or even broken bones. If your guinea pig

is injured, take them to the vet for evaluation and treatment. For minor injuries, you can clean the wound with a saline solution, but always follow your vet's advice for proper care.

4. Recovery: During recovery, ensure your guinea pig has a calm, quiet environment with plenty of fresh hay and vegetables. Monitor their progress and ensure they're eating and drinking properly.

FREQUENTLY ASKED QUESTIONS

1. How often should I take my guinea pig to the vet?

Guinea pigs should have a health check-up at least once a year, but more frequent visits may be necessary if they show signs of illness or injury.

2. Can guinea pigs live alone?

While guinea pigs can live alone, they are social animals and thrive in the company of other guinea pigs. If you only have one, be sure to spend plenty of time interacting with them daily.

3. How can I tell if my guinea pig is overweight?

Guinea pigs should have a healthy, well-proportioned body. If they have a rounded, bloated appearance or difficulty moving, they may be overweight. Consult your vet for proper weight management.

4. What is the best way to prevent health problems in guinea pigs?

Providing a balanced diet rich in fiber, regular vet check-ups, keeping their living space clean, and offering plenty of mental and physical stimulation are all key to keeping your guinea pig healthy.

5. Why is my guinea pig grinding its teeth?

Grinding teeth can be a sign of discomfort, stress, or pain, especially if accompanied by other symptoms. It may indicate dental problems or a health issue, so a vet visit is recommended. While guinea pigs are relatively easy to care for, it's essential to be aware of potential health issues, stress factors, and behaviors that may need attention. By staying observant, providing a calm environment, and addressing problems promptly, you can ensure your guinea pig remains happy and healthy.

CHAPTER FIVE

SENIOR GUINEA PIG CARE

As guinea pigs age, their needs evolve, and providing specialized care is essential to ensure they continue to lead a happy, healthy life. Just like humans, senior guinea pigs experience changes in their physical and emotional well-being. In this chapter, we'll explore how to care for older guinea pigs, recognize signs of aging, and provide comfort as they enter their senior years.

CARING FOR OLDER GUINEA PIGS

Older guinea pigs require special attention to maintain their quality of life. Their energy levels may decrease, and they may develop certain health conditions that require management. As a pet parent, it's important to adjust your care routine to meet their needs.

1. Regular Vet Check-Ups: Senior guinea pigs should visit the vet more frequently for check-ups, ideally every 6 months. Your vet will monitor their weight, check for any underlying health issues, and provide recommendations for dietary adjustments or supplements.

2. Modified Cage Setup: As guinea pigs age, they may experience mobility issues such as arthritis or a decrease in muscle strength. Ensure their cage is easy to access and has low barriers for easy entry. You may also want to add soft bedding or blankets to support their joints.

3. Increased Focus on Comfort: Older guinea pigs may sleep more often and require a quieter, more comfortable environment. Ensure they have plenty of soft bedding, hiding places, and cozy spots to rest.

4. Exercise Considerations: While older guinea pigs may not be as active, they still need gentle

exercise to maintain muscle tone and prevent obesity. Offer opportunities for light play and encourage activity by placing treats or toys within easy reach.

SIGNS OF AGING AND HEALTH CONCERNS

As guinea pigs get older, they can experience a range of health concerns. Recognizing the signs of aging and potential health problems is crucial for providing timely care.

1. Weight Loss: One of the most common signs of aging in guinea pigs is weight loss. Older guinea pigs may have a reduced appetite due to dental issues, gastrointestinal problems, or other health conditions. Regular weight checks will help you monitor changes and seek help if necessary.

2. Decreased Activity and Lethargy: Older guinea pigs may become less active and spend more time resting. While some reduction in activity is

normal, extreme lethargy could indicate underlying health issues, such as arthritis, dental pain, or organ failure.

3. Changes in Coat and Skin: An aging guinea pig may develop a duller or thinner coat, and their skin may become more fragile. If you notice excessive shedding, bald spots, or changes in their coat texture, it's important to consult with a vet to rule out health problems.

4. Difficulty Eating: Aging guinea pigs often experience dental issues, such as overgrown or misaligned teeth, which can make eating painful. If your guinea pig is having trouble eating, losing weight, or only eating soft foods, they may have dental problems.

5. Behavioral Changes: Older guinea pigs may become less social, more irritable, or less responsive to handling. These behavioral changes can be a sign of physical discomfort or health

issues, so it's important to observe and take action if needed.

6. Respiratory Issues: Like many other small animals, senior guinea pigs can be prone to respiratory infections. If you notice labored breathing, wheezing, or nasal discharge, take your guinea pig to the vet promptly for evaluation.

ADJUSTING THEIR DIET AND ENVIRONMENT

Older guinea pigs have different dietary needs than younger guinea pigs. Their digestion may slow down, and they may require more easily digestible food or supplements to stay healthy.

1. Dietary Adjustments:

Hay: Continue providing unlimited hay, as it's essential for digestion and dental health. However, older guinea pigs may benefit from softer hay, such as timothy hay, which is easier to chew.

Fresh Vegetables: Provide a variety of fresh vegetables, but avoid giving them too much high-calcium or high-oxalate foods (like spinach and kale) as they can contribute to urinary issues in senior guinea pigs.

Pellets: Look for senior guinea pig pellets that are formulated for their specific nutritional needs, including higher fiber content and lower protein levels.

Vitamin C: Senior guinea pigs still need plenty of Vitamin C for immunity and overall health. Provide vitamin C-rich foods like bell peppers and parsley or consider adding a vitamin C supplement if recommended by your vet.

2. Hydration: Older guinea pigs may have a reduced sense of thirst or difficulty drinking from water bottles. Ensure they have access to both

water bottles and bowls, and encourage them to drink regularly by offering water-rich vegetables like cucumber and leafy greens.

3. Environmental Modifications:

Comfortable Bedding: Older guinea pigs may benefit from soft, fleece bedding, which is gentler on their joints. Avoid bedding materials like cedar or pine, as they can irritate their respiratory system.

Temperature Regulation: Senior guinea pigs are more sensitive to extreme temperatures. Keep their environment cool in summer and warm in winter, and avoid sudden temperature fluctuations.

Ease of Movement: Make sure their cage is easy to navigate, with low barriers and smooth surfaces. You may also want to provide ramps or platforms that are easier to climb than tall, steep areas.

PROVIDING COMFORT FOR AGING GUINEA PIGS

Ensuring your senior guinea pig is comfortable requires attention to their physical and emotional needs. Consider these strategies for providing comfort in their later years:

1. Gentle Handling: Senior guinea pigs may become more fragile or sensitive to handling. Always support their body when picking them up and avoid rough handling. Be patient and gentle to reduce stress.

2. Cuddling and Bonding Time: While they may not be as active as they once were, your senior guinea pig will still enjoy regular interaction. Spend quiet time with them, offering cuddles or simply sitting with them to provide comfort and companionship.

3. Create a Calm Environment: Reduce the amount of noise, activity, and disruptions in their

living space. Senior guinea pigs often benefit from a calm, consistent routine that helps them feel safe and secure.

4. Monitor Their Health: Stay vigilant for any signs of discomfort, illness, or pain. If your guinea pig seems to be in distress, consult your vet promptly. Regularly check their weight, eating habits, and overall condition to stay ahead of any potential health issues.

END-OF-LIFE CARE AND SAYING GOODBYE

The end of life is a difficult time for both you and your guinea pig, but it's important to provide compassionate care in their final days. Knowing when it's time to say goodbye is never easy, but your guinea pig's comfort should be your top priority.

1. Recognizing When It's Time: If your guinea pig is in severe pain, stops eating or drinking entirely,

or is suffering from irreversible health conditions, it may be time to consider euthanasia. Your vet can help guide you through this decision and provide advice on how to handle the situation compassionately.

2. Making Their Final Days Comfortable: Focus on keeping your guinea pig as comfortable as possible. This may include offering their favorite foods, adjusting their cage to be more accessible, and providing extra warmth or quiet time to reduce stress.

3. Saying Goodbye: Saying goodbye to a beloved pet is never easy. Give your guinea pig a gentle and peaceful passing by offering them your love and attention during their final moments. Consider keeping a memento, such as a paw print or photo, to remember the special bond you shared.

In conclusion, senior guinea pig care requires patience, understanding, and commitment. With the right attention and adjustments to their diet, environment, and daily routine, you can ensure that your aging guinea pig remains comfortable and content. Although the end-of-life journey is never easy, providing a loving and compassionate environment in their final days will allow you to honor the life they shared with you.

GUINEA PIG MYTHS AND MISCONCEPTIONS

Guinea pigs are beloved pets, but they come with their fair share of myths and misconceptions that can confuse new pet owners. In this chapter, we'll explore some of the most common myths surrounding guinea pigs, debunk them, and provide the truth about their needs, housing, diet, and behavior.

DEBUNKING COMMON GUINEA PIG MYTHS

1. Guinea Pigs Are Low-Maintenance Pets

Myth: Many people believe guinea pigs are simple, low-maintenance pets that require little attention or care.

Reality: While guinea pigs are relatively easy to care for, they still require time, attention, and commitment. They need proper diet, daily care, social interaction, and a suitable living environment. Regular cleaning, exercise, and veterinary visits are all essential aspects of guinea pig care.

2. Guinea Pigs Can Live Alone and Don't Need Companions

Myth: Some believe guinea pigs can live happily by themselves without the need for social interaction.

Reality: Guinea pigs are social animals that thrive in pairs or small groups. In the wild, they live in herds, so having at least one companion is vital for their emotional well-being. If you must keep a single guinea pig, you'll need to provide more attention and interaction to ensure they don't become lonely or stressed.

3. Guinea Pigs Can Eat Just About Anything

Myth: Some people think guinea pigs can eat any type of vegetable, fruit, or food scraps.

Reality: Guinea pigs have very specific dietary needs. They require high-quality hay, fresh vegetables, and a small amount of pellets. They should never eat foods high in sugar, fat, or certain veggies like iceberg lettuce, which offers little nutritional value. Additionally, some foods like onions, garlic, and chocolate are toxic to guinea pigs.

4. Guinea Pigs Don't Need a Vet

Myth: Guinea pigs are often viewed as hardy animals that don't need regular veterinary care.

Reality: Guinea pigs require regular check-ups, especially as they age. They are prone to dental issues, respiratory infections, and other health problems that need professional attention. Early intervention is key to preventing serious health issues, so a vet familiar with guinea pigs is essential.

5. Guinea Pigs Are Noisy and Annoying

Myth: Some believe guinea pigs are constantly noisy and hard to tolerate because of their vocalizations.

Reality: While guinea pigs are vocal animals, their sounds are often cute and manageable. They "wheek" when excited or hungry, and make soft noises when content. With proper care and enrichment, they will be more relaxed and less likely to produce loud, excessive noise.

UNDERSTANDING GUINEA PIG NEEDS

Guinea pigs have unique needs when it comes to their diet, housing, and socialization. These needs are often misunderstood, which can lead to improper care.

1. Space and Housing

Myth: Guinea pigs can live in small cages, and they don't need much space.

Reality: Guinea pigs require ample space to roam and explore. The minimum recommended cage size for one guinea pig is 7.5 square feet, with additional space for each extra guinea pig. A larger cage encourages natural behaviors like running, burrowing, and socializing.

2. Exercise and Mental Stimulation

Myth: Guinea pigs don't need exercise because they're not very active.

Reality: Guinea pigs are naturally active creatures that need exercise to stay healthy. They should have time outside their cage to run around and explore in a safe, enclosed space. Providing them with toys and tunnels also helps to keep them mentally stimulated and engaged.

3. Socialization and Companionship

Myth: Guinea pigs can be kept alone if you give them enough attention.

Reality: Guinea pigs are highly social animals that need interaction with other guinea pigs or human companions. If you only have one guinea pig, they may become lonely or stressed, leading to behavioral issues. It's best to adopt guinea pigs in pairs or small groups to meet their social needs.

4. Lifespan

Myth: Guinea pigs only live a few years, so they're not a long-term commitment.

Reality: Guinea pigs typically live for 5 to 7 years, with some living even longer with proper care. This means they are a long-term commitment, requiring time, attention, and financial resources for their entire lifespan.

MYTHS ABOUT HOUSING, DIET, AND BEHAVIOR

Understanding the truth behind common misconceptions about guinea pig housing, diet, and behavior can help ensure that your pet thrives.

1. Guinea Pigs Can Live in Small, Closed-In Cages

Myth: Some owners believe that guinea pigs can be kept in small cages like hamster or rabbit enclosures.

Reality: Guinea pigs need larger, open spaces with room to move around. A small, closed cage can lead to stress, health problems, and unhappiness. Use a spacious cage with multiple levels, hideouts, and room for exercise. Ensure there's plenty of ventilation to avoid respiratory issues.

2. Guinea Pigs Don't Need Access to Fresh Water

Myth: It's okay to skip providing fresh water for guinea pigs, as they can live off the food they eat.

Reality: Guinea pigs need access to fresh, clean water at all times. Dehydration can lead to serious health issues, including kidney problems. Providing both a water bottle and a bowl ensures they stay hydrated.

3. Guinea Pigs Are Litter-Trained Like Cats

Myth: Some believe guinea pigs can be easily litter-trained and will always use a designated area.

Reality: While guinea pigs can be trained to use a certain area of their cage as a bathroom, they are not as reliable as cats when it comes to litter training. They may still "go" wherever they feel comfortable, so regular cleaning is essential to maintain a hygienic environment.

4. Guinea Pigs Don't Require Much Grooming

Myth: Guinea pigs are low-maintenance in terms of grooming and don't need regular care for their coats.

Reality: Guinea pigs, particularly long-haired breeds, need regular grooming to keep their coats healthy and free from mats. Even short-haired guinea pigs benefit from occasional brushing. Nail trimming and general hygiene are important parts of guinea pig care.

5. Guinea Pigs Don't Have Special Health Needs

Myth: Guinea pigs are tough animals that don't require any specialized health care.

Reality: Guinea pigs are prone to specific health issues like dental problems, gastrointestinal issues, and respiratory infections. Their diet, environment, and social needs should all be carefully managed to prevent health issues. Regular vet checkups are also important to ensure they stay healthy. There are many myths and misconceptions surrounding guinea pigs that can lead to confusion and inadequate care. By debunking these myths and understanding the true needs of guinea pigs, you can provide them with the best possible care. These small, social creatures deserve attention, space, proper diet, and a stimulating environment to thrive. With the right knowledge, you can ensure that your guinea pig leads a long, happy, and healthy life.

CHAPTER SIX

GUINEA PIG FUN FACTS AND INTERESTING INFORMATION

Guinea pigs are charming, delightful creatures with a rich history, an array of fascinating features, and a unique place in both culture and scientific research. In this chapter, we'll explore some fun and surprising facts about guinea pigs, dive into the various breeds and variations, look at their role in research and culture, and discover how these adorable animals have been represented in popular media.

FASCINATING FACTS ABOUT GUINEA PIGS

1. Guinea Pigs Are Not Pigs!

Despite their name, guinea pigs are not pigs, nor do they come from Guinea. They are rodents, belonging to the family Caviidae. Their full scientific name is Cavia porcellus. The name "guinea pig" is believed to have originated from their use as a form of currency in Guinea (a country in West Africa) and their pig-like squeals.

2. They Have Unique Vocalizations

Guinea pigs are quite vocal and communicate with a variety of sounds, each with its own meaning. They "wheek" when they're excited or want attention, make a "purring" sound when content, and may "chatter" their teeth when they're upset or threatened. Their wide range of vocalizations helps them interact with their surroundings and other guinea pigs.

3. Guinea Pigs Are Herbivores

Guinea pigs are strict herbivores, meaning they eat only plant-based foods. They primarily consume hay, vegetables, and fruits. Unlike many other rodents, guinea pigs cannot produce their own vitamin C, so they require a diet rich in this vitamin to stay healthy.

4. They Have No Tail

Guinea pigs are one of the few rodents that do not have a tail. This may seem unusual compared to other animals in the rodent family, but their lack of a tail doesn't hinder their balance or movement in any way.

5. Guinea Pigs Are Great Jumpers

Although guinea pigs are not known for climbing, they are actually quite good at jumping. They can leap up to a height of around two feet when they are startled or excited. So, it's essential to make sure their living space is safe and free from high ledges or gaps where they could hurt themselves.

6. Guinea Pigs Can Live a Long Time

On average, guinea pigs live for 5 to 7 years, but some can live up to 8 years or more with proper care. This relatively long lifespan for such small animals makes them a significant commitment for pet owners.

GUINEA PIG BREEDS AND VARIATIONS

Guinea pigs come in a variety of breeds, each with its own distinctive traits, such as coat types, colors, and personalities. Here are some of the most popular guinea pig breeds:

1. Abyssinian

Known for their short, curly coat that forms rosettes (swirls of hair), Abyssinians are lively and curious guinea pigs. They are one of the oldest and most recognizable guinea pig breeds.

2. Peruvian

Peruvian guinea pigs have long, silky hair that grows in a sweeping pattern down their backs. These guinea pigs require regular grooming to keep their coats looking beautiful and free of mats.

3. American

The American guinea pig is one of the most popular breeds, characterized by its short, smooth coat. They are friendly, social, and easy to handle, making them great pets for families.

4. Silkie (Sheltie)

Silkie guinea pigs have long, silky fur that flows from their body in a beautiful, smooth pattern. They require a lot of attention in terms of grooming to maintain their coat, but they are very affectionate and enjoy interacting with their owners.

5. Teddy

Teddy guinea pigs have a short, dense, and curly coat that gives them a teddy bear-like appearance.

They are known for being friendly, calm, and easy to handle.

6. Texel

Texel guinea pigs have a long, curly coat that is soft to the touch. These guinea pigs have a distinctive and unique look compared to other breeds, and they also require regular grooming.

7. Crested

Crested guinea pigs have a single tuft of hair on their head, known as the crest, which stands out from the rest of their fur. They come in both short-haired and long-haired varieties and are affectionate and playful pets.

THE ROLE OF GUINEA PIGS IN RESEARCH AND CULTURE

Guinea pigs have been used for centuries in scientific research and hold a special place in various cultures.

1. Guinea Pigs in Scientific Research

Guinea pigs have historically been used in laboratory research, especially in studies related to genetics, hearing, and nutrition. Their biological similarities to humans, such as their need for vitamin C, made them ideal subjects for early studies on human diseases and medicine. Today, they are still used in some areas of research, though their role has diminished with advances in technology and alternative testing methods.

2. Guinea Pigs in Ancient Cultures

In some South American cultures, guinea pigs have played an important role as both pets and a source of food. In the Andean region, they have been domesticated for thousands of years. They are considered a delicacy in some parts of Peru, Ecuador, and Bolivia, where they are traditionally prepared for special occasions.

3. Guinea Pigs in Modern Culture

Guinea pigs have made their way into popular culture as cute, lovable creatures. They are often featured in cartoons, children's books, and internet memes due to their endearing appearance and playful nature. Their presence in social media also contributes to their status as one of the most adored pets worldwide.

RECAP OF ESSENTIAL GUINEA PIG CARE TIPS

To summarize the key takeaways from this guide, here are the essential tips to remember when caring for your guinea pig:

1. Proper Housing and Environment

Choose a spacious cage that allows your guinea pig to move around freely and comfortably. Ensure the cage is equipped with soft bedding, and place it in a quiet, safe location away from direct sunlight and drafts.

Provide plenty of hiding spots, toys, and tunnels to encourage exploration and mental stimulation.

2. Balanced Diet

Guinea pigs are herbivores and require a steady diet of high-quality hay, fresh vegetables, and fruits. Vitamin C is essential for their health, so ensure they get enough through fresh produce or supplements.

Avoid feeding them sugary or fatty foods, as these can lead to health problems.

3. Regular Grooming and Hygiene

Depending on the breed, guinea pigs may require regular grooming. Long-haired breeds need frequent brushing to prevent their coats from tangling, while short-haired breeds only need occasional care.

Nail trimming, bathing, and brushing should be part of their regular hygiene routine.

4. Socialization and Handling

Guinea pigs are social animals and thrive when they have company, either from other guinea pigs or from human interaction. Handle your guinea pig gently and regularly to build trust and strengthen the bond.

Learn to read their body language to understand their emotions and make them feel safe and comfortable.

5. Health Monitoring and Veterinary Care

Regularly monitor your guinea pig for signs of illness such as changes in behavior, eating habits, or coat condition. Early detection of health issues can prevent more serious problems.

Schedule regular veterinary check-ups to ensure your guinea pig remains healthy and well-cared-for.

6. Play and Enrichment

Guinea pigs need mental stimulation and physical activity. Provide them with safe toys, tunnels, and plenty of space to explore. Encourage regular playtime outside their cage for enrichment.

NEXT STEPS IN YOUR GUINEA PIG JOURNEY

Now that you're equipped with the knowledge to care for your guinea pig, it's time to embark on your exciting journey as a guinea pig parent. Here are some next steps you can take to continue fostering a healthy, happy life for your pet:

1. Build a Strong Bond

Spend quality time with your guinea pig each day. Offer treats, talk to them, and engage in gentle play. Guinea pigs thrive on attention and affection from their owners.

2. Continue Learning

The world of guinea pig care is always evolving, so stay up to date with the latest information on guinea pig health, nutrition, and care. Follow guinea pig care websites, blogs, and social media accounts for ongoing advice and tips.

Join online guinea pig communities or local groups where you can connect with other guinea pig owners, share experiences, and ask for support.

3. Prepare for Future Stages

As your guinea pig grows older, their care needs may change. Pay close attention to their health and comfort as they age. Be prepared to make adjustments to their diet, habitat, and overall care to meet their evolving needs.

Keep in mind that guinea pigs typically live 5 to 7 years, but some can live even longer with proper care, so you'll need to be committed to their wellbeing for the long term.

4. Consider Adoption

If you're thinking about expanding your guinea pig family, consider adopting from a rescue shelter. There are many guinea pigs in need of loving homes, and adopting can be a rewarding experience for both you and the animal.

5. Respect Their Needs

Always respect your guinea pig's natural instincts. If your pet seems stressed, anxious, or scared, give them space and time to adjust. Understanding their behavior and needs will help you provide the best care possible. By following these steps and continuing to learn about guinea pig care, you'll ensure that your furry friend lives a fulfilling, healthy life. Guinea pigs are not just pets—they're companions that offer love, joy, and entertainment. With the right knowledge, you can make their world just as wonderful as they make yours. Enjoy your guinea pig journey!

Conclusion

As we reach the end of The Guinea Pig Guide: How to Raise, Feed, and Keep a Healthy Guinea Pig, we hope that you now feel more confident and knowledgeable in caring for these delightful, affectionate pets. Whether you're a first-time guinea pig owner or an experienced caregiver, the information in this book will help ensure that your guinea pig leads a happy, healthy life.